WELCOME TO THE FARM

Baler

Samantha Bell

Published in the United States of America
by Cherry Lake Publishing
Ann Arbor, Michigan
www.cherrylakepublishing.com

Content Adviser: Gary Powell, Weed Science Research Technician,
Michigan State University
Reading Adviser: Marla Conn MS, Ed., Literacy specialist, Read-Ability, Inc.
Photo Credits: © AGCO Corporation, all rights reserved, cover, 1, 2, 14, 18;
© Makaule/Shutterstock, 4; © Fotokostic/Shutterstock, 6;
© Polarpx/Shutterstock, 8; © Denton Rumsey/Shutterstock, 10;
© Skylines/Shutterstock, 12; © Helen's Photos/Shutterstock, 16;
© AVTG/istock, 20

Library of Congress Cataloging-in-Publication Data
Names: Bell, Samantha, author. | Bell, Samantha. Welcome to the farm.
Title: Baler / Samantha Bell.
Description: Ann Arbor : Cherry Lake Publishing, [2016] | Series: Welcome to
    the farm | Includes bibliographical references and index.
Identifiers: LCCN 2015047229| ISBN 9781634710374 (hardcover) |
    ISBN 9781634711364 (pdf) | ISBN 9781634712354 (pbk.) |
    ISBN 9781634713344 (ebook)
Subjects: LCSH: Agricultural machinery—Juvenile literature.
Classification: LCC S675.25 .B44 2016 | DDC 631.3—dc23
LC record available at http://lccn.loc.gov/2015047229

Cherry Lake Publishing would like to acknowledge the work of the Partnership
for 21st Century Skills. Please visit www.p21.org for more information.

Printed in the United States of America
Corporate Graphics

Table of Contents

Machines That Help

Balers are machines. They tie crops together in **bales**. The bales can be round or square. This baler is making big round bales of straw.

The bales can be moved with a tractor. They can be stored.

Things to Bale

Some balers bale corn **stalks**. Some bale hay. Some bale straw. Some bale cotton.

What is cotton used for?

These cotton bales are round. Sometimes they are square. Straw bales can also be round or square.

Time for Baling

This field has wheat straw. The farmer is ready for it to be baled. The straw is cut. It is on the ground.

Where does the driver sit?

The baler picks up the hay. It goes to the bale **chamber**. The hay is packed into a bale.

Ready to Go!

Some bales are tied with **twine**. Some are wrapped in plastic.

The baler drops the bale onto the ground. It starts a new one.

The bales are ready to go!

Find Out More

Roberts, Josephine. *Total Tractor!* New York: DK Publishing, 2015.

Massey Ferguson
www.masseyferguson.us/videos/massey-ferguson-2800-baler-animation.html
Watch an animated video of a round hay baler.

Glossary

bales (BAYLZ) large bundles of goods tied together (noun); ties a large bundle of goods together (verb)
chamber (CHAYM-bur) an enclosed space
stalks (STAWKS) plant stems
twine (TWYNE) a string made of two or more stands twisted together

Home and School Connection

Use this list of words from the book to help your child become a better reader. Word games and writing activities can help beginning readers reinforce literacy skills.

a	drops	onto	things
also	farmer	or	this
are	field	packed	tie
bale	for	picks	tied
baled	goes	plastic	time
baler	ground	ready	to
balers	has	round	together
bales	hay	sit	tractor
baling	help	some	twine
be	in	sometimes	up
big	into	square	used
can	is	stalks	what
chamber	it	starts	wheat
corn	machines	stored	where
cotton	making	straw	with
crops	moved	that	wrapped
cut	new	the	
does	of	these	
driver	one	they	

Index

About the Author

Samantha Bell is a children's book writer, illustrator, teacher, and mom of four busy kids. Her articles, short stories, and poems have been published online and in print.